We hope this book has been informative and helpful on your journey to understanding and celebrating older adults. Thank you for your interest and support!

Title: The Joy of Mindful Consumption
Subtitle: Finding Happiness in Less Stuff

Series: The Joy of Less: A Minimalist's Guide to Happiness

By Lily J. Thompson

"Minimalism is not a lack of something. It's simply the perfect amount of something."

Nicholas Burroughs

"Minimalism is not a style, it is an attitude, a way of being. It's a fundamental reaction against noise, visual noise, disorder, vulgarity. Minimalism is the pursuit of the essence of things, not the appearance."

Claudio Silvestrin

"Minimalism is the intentional promotion of the things we most value and the removal of anything that distracts us from it."

Joshua Becker

"Simplicity is the ultimate sophistication."

Leonardo da Vinci

"The ability to simplify means to eliminate the unnecessary so that the necessary may speak."

Hans Hofmann

"Minimalism is not a lack of personality, it's a matter of emphasizing what's important."

Unknown

"Minimalism is not about living in a stark, empty space. It's about surrounding yourself with the things you love and use most often."

Unknown

Table of Contents

Introduction

Defining minimalism and its origins

Minimalism is a lifestyle and mindset that emphasizes the value of simplicity, focusing on the things that matter most while letting go of excess and unnecessary clutter. The roots of minimalism can be traced back to various philosophical and artistic movements throughout history, but the modern concept of minimalism as a lifestyle has gained popularity in recent years.

At its core, minimalism is about living intentionally and with purpose, making deliberate choices about what we consume and how we spend our time and resources. This includes simplifying our possessions, reducing our environmental impact, and cultivating meaningful relationships and experiences.

The origins of modern minimalism can be attributed to a variety of factors, including the rise of consumerism and materialism in Western societies, as well as a growing awareness of the impact of our actions on the environment and society as a whole.

Some key figures in the minimalist movement include Joshua Fields Millburn and Ryan Nicodemus, who co-founded the website The Minimalists and have written several books on the topic, including "Minimalism: Live a

Meaningful Life." Other influential voices include Marie Kondo, the Japanese organizing consultant who popularized the concept of decluttering and sparked a global movement, and Fumio Sasaki, who wrote the book "Goodbye, Things: The New Japanese Minimalism."

While minimalism can mean different things to different people, at its core it is about finding happiness and fulfillment through less, rather than more. By simplifying our lives and reducing our consumption, we can create space for the things that truly matter and find greater peace and contentment in the process.

The rise of minimalism globally

Minimalism has become a global phenomenon in recent years, as more and more people seek to simplify their lives and reduce their consumption. The rise of minimalism can be attributed to a variety of factors, including environmental concerns, financial pressures, and a desire for greater well-being and fulfillment.

One of the key drivers of the global minimalist movement has been the growing awareness of the environmental impact of our consumption. As we become more conscious of the finite resources of our planet and the damage caused by waste and pollution, many people are turning to minimalism as a way to reduce their carbon footprint and live more sustainably. By embracing a minimalist lifestyle, we can reduce our reliance on single-use plastics, limit our consumption of meat and dairy products, and support sustainable fashion and products.

Another factor contributing to the rise of minimalism is the financial pressures facing many people in the wake of economic instability and rising inequality. By simplifying our possessions and focusing on the things that truly matter, we can save money, reduce debt, and live more frugally. This can be especially important for those struggling to make ends meet or facing financial insecurity.

Beyond environmental and financial concerns, the global minimalist movement is also driven by a desire for greater well-being and fulfillment. Many people find that simplifying their lives and reducing their consumption leads to a greater sense of peace, contentment, and purpose. By letting go of excess and focusing on what truly matters, we can create space for the things that bring us joy and fulfillment, such as meaningful relationships, creative pursuits, and personal growth.

The rise of minimalism has been fueled by a growing number of voices and communities advocating for a simpler, more intentional way of life. From popular bloggers and authors to social media influencers and documentary filmmakers, there are many voices championing the benefits of minimalism and inspiring others to adopt this lifestyle. The global reach of the internet and social media has made it easier than ever for people to connect with like-minded individuals and access resources and support for their minimalist journey.

In summary, the rise of minimalism globally reflects a growing awareness of the environmental impact of our consumption, financial pressures, and a desire for greater well-being and fulfillment. With the support of a vibrant and growing community, more and more people are embracing this lifestyle and discovering the benefits of a simpler, more intentional way of life.

Benefits of minimalism, including reducing stress, saving money, and reducing environmental impact

Minimalism is a lifestyle that is becoming increasingly popular around the world. It involves simplifying your life by reducing clutter and excess possessions, and focusing on the things that truly matter. There are many benefits to living a minimalist lifestyle, including reducing stress, saving money, and reducing your impact on the environment.

One of the most significant benefits of minimalism is that it can reduce stress and improve your overall well-being. By simplifying your surroundings and reducing the number of possessions you own, you can create a more calming and peaceful living environment. This can help to reduce feelings of anxiety and overwhelm, and allow you to focus on the things that are truly important in your life. By freeing up mental and physical space, you can also increase your productivity, creativity, and focus.

Another benefit of minimalism is that it can help you save money. By focusing on the things that truly matter, you can reduce your spending on unnecessary items and experiences. This can be especially important in today's economy, where many people are struggling to make ends meet. By living a more frugal and intentional lifestyle, you can reduce your debt, save for the future, and increase your financial security.

Minimalism can also have a positive impact on the environment. By reducing your consumption and waste, you can help to reduce your carbon footprint and limit the damage caused by climate change. This can be achieved by making conscious choices about the products you buy and the way you live your life. For example, you can reduce your use of single-use plastics, buy second-hand clothing, and choose products that are made from sustainable materials.

In addition to these benefits, minimalism can also lead to greater happiness and fulfillment. By focusing on the things that truly matter in your life, such as relationships, experiences, and personal growth, you can create a more meaningful and purposeful existence. By living with intention and purpose, you can cultivate a greater sense of joy and satisfaction in your life.

In summary, minimalism offers many benefits, including reducing stress, saving money, and reducing your impact on the environment. By simplifying your life and focusing on the things that truly matter, you can create a more meaningful and fulfilling existence. Whether you're looking to reduce your stress levels, improve your finances, or live a more sustainable life, minimalism offers a pathway towards a happier, more intentional way of living.

Chapter 1: Minimalist Living
Embracing a minimalist approach to home decor and design

Embracing a minimalist approach to home decor and design can be a powerful tool to simplify and streamline your living space. Instead of filling your home with unnecessary clutter and knick-knacks, a minimalist approach prioritizes clean lines, functional furniture, and only the essential decor items that bring you joy.

One of the key principles of minimalist home design is the idea of "less is more." This means that you should aim to have only the items that you truly need or love in your home, rather than filling it with things that simply take up space. When it comes to furniture, choose pieces that are functional and versatile, with a clean and simple aesthetic. This will help you create a space that feels open and uncluttered.

Another important aspect of minimalist home design is organization. By keeping your home organized and tidy, you can reduce stress and create a sense of calm. Use storage solutions like baskets, shelves, and bins to keep your belongings organized and out of sight. This will help you create a space that feels open and uncluttered, even if you have limited square footage.

When it comes to decor, a minimalist approach focuses on simplicity and functionality. Choose decor items that serve a purpose, such as a statement piece of artwork or a vase of fresh flowers, rather than cluttering your space with unnecessary trinkets. Additionally, a minimalist approach to decor means choosing a neutral color palette and avoiding bold patterns or prints. This can help create a sense of calm and serenity in your living space.

Ultimately, embracing a minimalist approach to home decor and design can help you create a living space that is both functional and beautiful. By prioritizing simplicity and organization, you can reduce stress, increase productivity, and create a sense of calm in your home.

Simplifying your living space

Simplifying your living space is a key component of minimalist living, and can help you reduce stress, increase productivity, and create a sense of calm in your home.

One of the first steps to simplifying your living space is to declutter. Go through each room in your home and get rid of anything that is no longer useful or doesn't bring you joy. This can include old clothes, broken appliances, and decor items that no longer serve a purpose. By reducing the amount of stuff in your home, you'll have more space to move around and breathe, and can better appreciate the items that you do choose to keep.

Once you've decluttered, it's important to organize your remaining belongings in a way that makes sense for your lifestyle. This can include using storage solutions like baskets, shelves, and bins to keep your items organized and out of sight. Be sure to keep items that you use frequently in easy-to-reach places, while storing less frequently used items in a designated storage area.

When it comes to furniture, choose pieces that are functional and versatile. For example, a sofa that doubles as a guest bed or a storage ottoman can be a great way to maximize space and reduce clutter. Additionally, consider investing in multifunctional pieces like a folding dining table or a wall-mounted desk, which can be used when needed and then easily tucked away.

Another important aspect of simplifying your living space is to keep your decor simple and functional. Choose items that serve a purpose, such as a statement piece of artwork or a vase of fresh flowers, rather than cluttering your space with unnecessary trinkets. Additionally, a minimalist approach to decor means choosing a neutral color palette and avoiding bold patterns or prints.

By simplifying your living space, you'll be able to create a sense of calm and serenity in your home. You'll have more space to move around and breathe, and can better appreciate the items that you do choose to keep. Ultimately, a simplified living space can help you live a happier, more intentional life.

Incorporating minimalism into your daily routine

Incorporating minimalism into your daily routine is all about simplifying your life and making more time for the things that matter most to you. Here are some practical tips for incorporating minimalism into your daily routine:

1. Practice mindfulness: Mindfulness is the practice of being present in the moment and paying attention to your thoughts and surroundings without judgment. Practicing mindfulness can help you be more intentional about how you spend your time and reduce the impulse to constantly check your phone or engage in other distracting activities.

2. Develop a morning routine: A morning routine can help you start your day with intention and focus. Some ideas for a minimalist morning routine include meditation, yoga, journaling, or simply taking a few minutes to sit quietly and reflect on your day.

3. Plan your day: Taking a few minutes each morning to plan your day can help you stay on track and avoid getting overwhelmed by a long to-do list. Prioritize the most important tasks and schedule time for self-care and relaxation.

4. Declutter regularly: Regularly decluttering your living space can help you feel more organized and reduce

stress. Set aside time each week to go through your belongings and get rid of items you no longer need or use.

5. Practice digital minimalism: Digital minimalism is the practice of using technology in a way that supports your values and goals. Set boundaries around your phone and social media use, and consider deleting apps or unfollowing accounts that don't add value to your life.

6. Create a minimalist wardrobe: A minimalist wardrobe is one that is intentionally curated with a few high-quality, versatile pieces. Consider donating or selling clothes you no longer wear and focus on building a wardrobe that makes you feel confident and comfortable.

7. Embrace slow living: Slow living is the practice of slowing down and being more intentional with your time. This can include activities like cooking, reading, or spending time in nature. Embracing slow living can help you feel more relaxed and connected to the world around you.

By incorporating these simple practices into your daily routine, you can live a more minimalist lifestyle and create more space in your life for the things that truly matter.

Benefits of a minimalist home

A minimalist home can provide many benefits, both practical and emotional. By simplifying your living space, you can reduce stress, save money, and create a more peaceful environment for yourself and your family. Here are some of the key benefits of a minimalist home:

1. Less clutter and more space: By getting rid of unnecessary possessions and focusing only on what you truly need and value, you can create more physical space in your home. This can help you feel more relaxed and less overwhelmed by the chaos of clutter.

2. Easier cleaning and maintenance: With fewer items to clean and maintain, you can spend less time on household chores and more time on things that matter to you, such as spending time with loved ones or pursuing hobbies.

3. More financial freedom: By avoiding the temptation to constantly buy new things and instead focusing on what you truly need, you can save money and achieve greater financial freedom. This can also help you avoid the stress of debt and financial worry.

4. Enhanced focus and creativity: A minimalist home can create a sense of calm and focus that allows you to be more productive and creative. With fewer distractions and

visual clutter, you can focus more easily on your work or other goals.

5. Greater peace of mind: By simplifying your living space and possessions, you can create a more peaceful and calming environment. This can help reduce stress and anxiety, allowing you to feel more centered and grounded.

Overall, a minimalist home can provide many benefits, both practical and emotional. By embracing a minimalist approach to your living space, you can create a more peaceful, calm, and enjoyable environment for yourself and your family.

Chapter 2: Minimalist Eating
Simplifying your diet and meal planning

Eating a healthy and balanced diet is essential for maintaining good health, but it can be overwhelming to navigate the vast array of food choices available to us. Simplifying your diet and meal planning is one way to alleviate this stress and ensure that you are getting the nutrients you need without overcomplicating things.

To begin simplifying your diet, start by focusing on whole, unprocessed foods. This means avoiding pre-packaged and processed foods, which often contain high amounts of salt, sugar, and unhealthy fats. Instead, opt for fresh fruits and vegetables, whole grains, lean proteins, and healthy fats.

One approach to meal planning that can help simplify your diet is to choose a few staple meals that you enjoy and rotate them throughout the week. This takes the guesswork out of meal planning and allows you to streamline your grocery shopping and food preparation. For example, you might have a few go-to meals such as roasted vegetables and chicken, quinoa bowls, or stir-fry dishes that you make regularly.

Another strategy for simplifying your diet is to meal prep in advance. This means preparing a week's worth of meals in advance and storing them in the refrigerator or freezer for easy access throughout the week. Meal prepping saves time and money, and ensures that you always have healthy options on hand.

In addition to simplifying your diet, it's also important to pay attention to portion sizes. Eating too much of even healthy foods can lead to overconsumption of calories, which can contribute to weight gain and other health problems. Using smaller plates, measuring out serving sizes, and paying attention to your body's hunger cues can all help you to eat in moderation.

By simplifying your diet and meal planning, you can reduce stress around food choices and ensure that you are getting the nutrients you need for good health. Additionally, eating a diet rich in whole, unprocessed foods can help reduce your environmental impact by reducing packaging waste and promoting sustainable agriculture practices.

Reducing food waste and minimizing packaging waste

Reducing food waste and minimizing packaging waste are important aspects of minimalist eating that not only benefit the environment but also help save money. When we waste food, we not only throw away money, but also contribute to greenhouse gas emissions from landfills. Similarly, when we buy food packaged in excessive or non-recyclable materials, we add to the growing problem of plastic pollution.

Here are some tips for reducing food and packaging waste in a minimalist diet:

1. Plan meals and shop intentionally: Plan your meals for the week before you go grocery shopping. This will help you buy only what you need and reduce the likelihood of food waste. Make a list of the ingredients you need and stick to it. When you're at the store, avoid buying in bulk unless you know you'll use all of it.

2. Buy in-season produce: Not only is in-season produce often cheaper, it's also likely to be fresher and have a lower carbon footprint because it doesn't have to travel as far to get to you.

3. Store food properly: Proper storage can extend the life of your food and reduce waste. For example, keep

vegetables in the crisper drawer of your fridge and keep bread in the freezer to prevent it from going stale.

4. Use leftovers creatively: Don't let leftovers go to waste! Incorporate them into new meals or freeze them for later. You can also use vegetable scraps to make broth or compost them.

5. Avoid excessive packaging: Look for foods with minimal packaging, or choose items that come in recyclable or biodegradable packaging. Bring reusable bags, containers, and utensils when shopping or getting takeout.

By reducing food and packaging waste, we not only live a more minimalist lifestyle, but also contribute to a healthier planet.

The benefits of a minimalist approach to eating for health and the environment

Adopting a minimalist approach to eating can have numerous benefits for both your health and the environment. Here are some of the key benefits:

1. Improved health: Minimalist eating involves focusing on whole, unprocessed foods that are rich in nutrients. This can help improve your overall health by providing your body with the nutrients it needs to function optimally. Additionally, a minimalist approach to eating can help you maintain a healthy weight, reduce your risk of chronic diseases, and improve your digestion.

2. Reduced environmental impact: Eating a minimalist diet can also help reduce your environmental impact. By choosing foods that are in season and grown locally, you can reduce the carbon footprint associated with transporting food long distances. Additionally, by choosing foods that are grown using sustainable farming practices, you can help reduce the environmental impact associated with conventional farming methods.

3. Reduced food waste: Minimalist eating also involves reducing food waste. By planning your meals carefully and only buying what you need, you can help reduce the amount of food that goes to waste. Additionally,

by composting food scraps and using them to enrich your soil, you can help reduce the amount of food waste that ends up in landfills.

4. Reduced packaging waste: A minimalist approach to eating can also help reduce packaging waste. By choosing foods that are minimally packaged or packaged in recyclable materials, you can help reduce the amount of waste that ends up in landfills.

5. Cost savings: Finally, minimalist eating can also help you save money. By focusing on whole, unprocessed foods, you can reduce your reliance on expensive processed foods and supplements. Additionally, by reducing food waste and buying only what you need, you can help reduce your grocery bill.

Overall, adopting a minimalist approach to eating can have numerous benefits for both your health and the environment. By focusing on whole, unprocessed foods, reducing food and packaging waste, and choosing foods that are grown sustainably and locally, you can help improve your health and reduce your environmental impact.

The impact of food choices on the environment and animals

The impact of our food choices goes far beyond just our personal health. What we choose to eat has a significant impact on the environment and the animals that inhabit it. In recent years, there has been growing concern over the environmental impact of food production and the treatment of animals in the industry. By adopting a minimalist approach to eating, we can reduce our impact and make more conscious choices.

One of the primary environmental impacts of our food choices is greenhouse gas emissions. The production, transportation, and packaging of food contribute significantly to carbon emissions, which are a major driver of climate change. In particular, animal agriculture is a significant contributor to greenhouse gas emissions, with livestock production accounting for around 14.5% of all human-caused emissions. By reducing our consumption of animal products, we can help to reduce our personal carbon footprint and contribute to the fight against climate change.

In addition to greenhouse gas emissions, the production of animal products also has significant land and water use impacts. Animal agriculture requires large amounts of land and water resources, which can lead to deforestation, desertification, and water scarcity in certain regions. By reducing our consumption of animal products, we can help to conserve these resources and reduce the pressure on the environment.

Another important consideration when it comes to food choices is the treatment of animals in the industry. Many people are becoming more aware of the ethical implications of consuming animal products, as well as the potential health risks associated with consuming meat from animals that have been treated with antibiotics and hormones. By reducing our consumption of animal products, we can support more ethical and sustainable farming practices and contribute to the welfare of animals.

In addition to the environmental and ethical benefits of a minimalist approach to eating, there are also potential health benefits. A diet that is high in fruits, vegetables, whole grains, and plant-based protein sources has been associated with a lower risk of chronic diseases such as heart disease, diabetes, and certain types of cancer. By reducing our consumption of processed and high-calorie foods, we can improve our overall health and wellbeing.

Overall, the impact of our food choices extends far beyond our personal health. By adopting a minimalist approach to eating and reducing our consumption of animal products, we can help to reduce our environmental impact, support more ethical and sustainable farming practices, and improve our overall health and wellbeing.

Chapter 3: Minimalist Materials
The impact of consumerism on the environment

Consumerism has become a way of life for many people, particularly in developed countries. It is a culture where people prioritize buying and owning more things, regardless of their actual needs. While consumerism has provided economic benefits, it has also led to several negative impacts on the environment.

One of the most significant environmental impacts of consumerism is the increase in waste. As people buy more products, they also generate more waste, particularly non-biodegradable waste, such as plastic. According to the United Nations Environment Programme, about 300 million tons of plastic waste are generated globally every year, with only about 9% of it being recycled. The rest ends up in landfills, oceans, and other natural environments, causing significant harm to wildlife and ecosystems.

Consumerism also contributes to the depletion of natural resources. The production of goods requires raw materials, and the more people consume, the more natural resources are needed. Many of these resources are finite and non-renewable, such as oil, coal, and natural gas. The extraction of these resources often results in significant damage to the environment, including deforestation, water pollution, and soil erosion.

Another significant impact of consumerism is the greenhouse gas emissions associated with the production and transportation of goods. The manufacturing process of many products requires significant amounts of energy, primarily from fossil fuels. Transportation, whether it be by land, sea, or air, also requires fossil fuels and generates greenhouse gas emissions that contribute to climate change.

In addition to the environmental impacts, consumerism also has social impacts. Companies often use unethical practices, such as exploiting workers and communities in developing countries to produce goods at a lower cost. Consumers are also often bombarded with marketing messages that create a desire for more things, leading to a cycle of constant consumption.

In summary, consumerism has significant negative impacts on the environment, including increased waste, depletion of natural resources, and greenhouse gas emissions. It also has social impacts, including exploitation of workers and communities and the creation of a culture of constant consumption. A minimalist approach to consumption can help reduce these impacts by prioritizing only what is necessary and meaningful, rather than buying and owning more things for the sake of it.

Reducing waste and promoting sustainability

As we continue to consume at an unprecedented rate, we generate an enormous amount of waste that can have long-lasting and harmful effects on the environment. However, by adopting a minimalist approach to materials, we can reduce our waste and promote sustainability.

One of the key ways to reduce waste is by reusing and repurposing items instead of buying new ones. By finding new uses for old items, we can keep them out of landfills and reduce the demand for new products. For example, instead of buying new clothes, we can mend and alter the ones we have to extend their lifespan. We can also donate or sell items we no longer need or want to give them a new life with someone else.

Another way to promote sustainability is by choosing products that are made with eco-friendly materials or that have been produced using sustainable manufacturing methods. For example, we can opt for products made from renewable resources, such as bamboo or recycled materials, and choose brands that have made a commitment to reducing their environmental impact.

We can also reduce waste by being mindful of our consumption habits. By making a conscious effort to only buy what we need and avoid impulse purchases, we can reduce the amount of waste we generate. We can also choose products with minimal packaging and recycle any packaging that we do receive.

Finally, we can make a difference by supporting companies and organizations that are committed to promoting sustainability and reducing waste. By using our purchasing power to support environmentally responsible businesses, we can encourage more companies to adopt sustainable practices.

In conclusion, by adopting a minimalist approach to materials, we can reduce our waste and promote sustainability. Whether it's by reusing and repurposing items, choosing eco-friendly products, or being mindful of our consumption habits, we can all make a difference in reducing our impact on the environment.

Ethical consumerism and the impact of our purchasing decisions

When we go shopping, we often consider factors such as price, quality, and convenience. However, we may not always think about the ethical implications of our purchases. Ethical consumerism is the idea that we should make purchasing decisions based on values such as sustainability, fair labor practices, and animal welfare. By practicing ethical consumerism, we can make a positive impact on the world around us.

The impact of our purchasing decisions can be significant. For example, the clothing industry is one of the largest polluters in the world, with the production of textiles accounting for approximately 10% of global carbon emissions. Fast fashion, which refers to the trend of quickly producing and selling inexpensive clothing, contributes to this problem by encouraging consumers to purchase and dispose of clothing at an alarming rate.

By choosing to purchase clothing made from sustainable materials such as organic cotton or recycled fabrics, we can reduce our impact on the environment. Additionally, purchasing clothing from companies that prioritize fair labor practices can help to support workers who may otherwise be exploited.

Similarly, when it comes to food, ethical consumerism can have a significant impact. By choosing to purchase organic, locally-sourced, or fair trade products, we can support sustainable agriculture and fair labor practices. We can also reduce the impact of factory farming on the environment and improve animal welfare.

Another area where ethical consumerism can make a difference is in the realm of electronics. The production of electronics relies on the mining of minerals such as coltan, which is often sourced from conflict zones where human rights abuses occur. By choosing to purchase electronics from companies that prioritize ethical sourcing practices, we can help to reduce our impact on these areas of conflict and support ethical labor practices.

Overall, ethical consumerism is about making purchasing decisions that align with our values and have a positive impact on the world around us. By considering factors such as sustainability, fair labor practices, and animal welfare when making purchases, we can help to promote a more just and equitable world.

Minimalist approaches to fashion and personal style

When it comes to minimalist living, one area where many people can make significant changes is in their approach to fashion and personal style. Fast fashion and trends have led to a culture of overconsumption, where we're buying more clothes than we need and discarding them at an alarming rate. In this chapter, we'll explore minimalist approaches to fashion and personal style that can help you reduce waste, save money, and feel more confident in your appearance.

What is Minimalist Fashion?

Minimalist fashion is about creating a wardrobe of high-quality, versatile pieces that can be mixed and matched to create a variety of different outfits. The goal is to have a smaller number of clothes that you really love and wear regularly, rather than a large number of items that you hardly ever touch. By investing in timeless, well-made pieces that can be worn for years to come, you'll save money and reduce waste.

How to Build a Minimalist Wardrobe

Building a minimalist wardrobe involves taking a thoughtful, intentional approach to your clothing choices. Here are some steps to follow:

1. Evaluate your current wardrobe. Start by taking everything out of your closet and dresser and sorting it into piles: keep, donate, and sell. Be honest with yourself about what you actually wear and what you can live without.

2. Identify your personal style. What types of clothes do you feel most comfortable and confident in? What colors and patterns do you prefer? Use this information to create a basic style profile that you can reference when shopping.

3. Invest in high-quality basics. Basics are the foundation of any minimalist wardrobe, so invest in high-quality pieces that will stand the test of time. This might include things like a well-fitted pair of jeans, a white button-up shirt, and a classic trench coat.

4. Choose versatile pieces. Look for items that can be dressed up or down, worn in different seasons, and paired with multiple other pieces in your wardrobe. For example, a simple black dress can be worn with sandals in the summer or layered with a sweater and boots in the winter.

5. Avoid trends. Trends come and go, so it's best to avoid them when building a minimalist wardrobe. Stick to classic, timeless styles that you know you'll wear for years to come.

Sustainable Fashion

In addition to being minimalist, it's also important to consider the sustainability of your clothing choices. The fashion industry is one of the biggest polluters in the world, and many popular clothing brands rely on sweatshops and exploitative labor practices to produce their garments.

To make more sustainable fashion choices, consider shopping at second-hand stores or investing in ethical, sustainable clothing brands. Look for certifications like Fair Trade or GOTS (Global Organic Textile Standard) to ensure that the clothes you buy are made under fair and sustainable conditions.

The Benefits of Minimalist Fashion

There are many benefits to adopting a minimalist approach to fashion and personal style. Here are just a few:

1. Saves money. By investing in high-quality pieces that you'll wear for years, you'll ultimately spend less money on clothing over time.

2. Reduces waste. By buying less and choosing sustainable, ethically-made clothing, you'll help reduce the amount of textile waste that ends up in landfills.

3. Saves time. When you have a smaller, more intentional wardrobe, getting dressed in the morning becomes easier and quicker.

4. Boosts confidence. When you're wearing clothes that you love and feel good in, it can boost your confidence and self-esteem.

5. Reduces decision fatigue. By having a smaller wardrobe with fewer choices, you'll reduce decision fatigue and free up mental space for more important decisions.

Overall, adopting a minimalist approach to fashion and personal style can be a powerful way to simplify your life, save money, and reduce your environmental impact. By embracing a minimalist wardrobe, you can cut down on clutter and the stress that comes with having too many choices. You can focus on owning fewer, high-quality items that you truly love and feel comfortable in. This approach can also help you develop a better understanding of your personal style and what truly suits you, leading to more confidence and less time spent worrying about what to wear. Additionally, by choosing sustainable and ethical fashion options, you can reduce the negative impact of the fashion industry on the environment and on workers in developing countries. By choosing to invest in well-made, timeless pieces, you can create a wardrobe that lasts longer, reducing the amount of clothing waste that ends up in landfills. Overall, minimalist fashion is not only better for the environment and for workers in the fashion industry, but it can also lead to a more fulfilling and stress-free personal style.

Chapter 4: Minimalist People
The benefits of cultivating meaningful relationships

Cultivating meaningful relationships is essential for leading a fulfilling life, and adopting a minimalist approach can help to prioritize and strengthen these connections. By focusing on quality over quantity, we can build deeper, more authentic relationships with the people who matter most to us. In a world where social media and technology often dominate our interactions, taking the time to connect with loved ones face-to-face and invest in shared experiences can be incredibly rewarding. Meaningful relationships provide a sense of belonging, emotional support, and the opportunity to share our joys and challenges with others. These relationships can also provide us with a sense of purpose and meaning in life, as we work together to support and encourage one another. Whether it's through family, friends, or community involvement, cultivating meaningful relationships can bring tremendous benefits to our mental health, emotional wellbeing, and overall quality of life.

Setting boundaries and simplifying your social life

Setting boundaries and simplifying your social life are essential aspects of minimalist living. It involves prioritizing quality over quantity and ensuring that your social connections align with your values and goals. Here are some tips for setting boundaries and simplifying your social life:

1. Evaluate your current social connections: Take a step back and assess the people in your life. Are these relationships meaningful and aligned with your values? If not, consider limiting or ending them.

2. Practice saying no: Learn to say no to invitations, events, or activities that don't align with your priorities. It's okay to decline an invitation that doesn't serve your needs or align with your goals.

3. Create a social calendar: Keep track of social events, gatherings, and activities that you enjoy and are aligned with your goals. Limit the number of social engagements in your calendar and prioritize the most meaningful ones.

4. Simplify your social media: Limit your social media use and unfollow accounts that do not serve your well-being or contribute to your personal growth.

5. Cultivate meaningful relationships: Focus on nurturing and investing in relationships that matter to you. Spend time with people who share similar values and

interests, and who support your personal growth and development.

By setting boundaries and simplifying your social life, you can reduce stress, increase your well-being, and cultivate deeper connections with those who matter most to you. Minimalist living is about living intentionally and focusing on what truly matters, and this applies to our social lives as well.

Letting go of toxic relationships and negative influences

In our lives, we come across different kinds of people, some of whom bring positivity and happiness, while others may have a negative influence on our well-being. A minimalist approach to relationships involves letting go of toxic relationships and negative influences that no longer serve us. This can be a difficult but necessary step towards a happier and more fulfilling life. It can be challenging to identify toxic relationships and negative influences, but some signs include constant criticism, manipulation, disrespect, and draining your energy and time.

Letting go of such relationships and influences can be difficult, especially when they involve people we care about. However, holding onto such relationships can be harmful to our mental and emotional health. We need to surround ourselves with people who support us and encourage personal growth, rather than those who drag us down or hold us back.

It's important to set boundaries to protect ourselves from negative influences, whether it's saying no to activities that drain our energy or limiting our exposure to certain people. Setting boundaries may involve having honest and uncomfortable conversations with people in our lives, but it's necessary for our well-being. It's okay to prioritize ourselves and our mental health, even if it means distancing ourselves from certain people.

By letting go of toxic relationships and negative influences and setting boundaries, we create space for positive relationships and experiences in our lives. We can cultivate deeper and more meaningful connections with people who bring joy and positivity into our lives, and focus on building healthy and supportive relationships. Ultimately, the minimalist approach to relationships is about prioritizing our well-being and happiness by surrounding ourselves with people who uplift us and add value to our lives.

Building community and finding support in a minimalist lifestyle

Living a minimalist lifestyle can be a lonely experience if you don't have a community or support system to lean on. Building a community of like-minded individuals who share your values can make a huge difference in your journey towards simplicity. There are many ways to find support and build a community around minimalism. Here are a few ideas to get started:

1. Join online communities: There are many online communities dedicated to minimalism, such as forums, Facebook groups, and subreddits. Joining these communities can be a great way to connect with others who are on a similar journey and share tips and advice.

2. Attend events and meetups: Look for local events and meetups focused on minimalism, such as talks, workshops, or even minimalist markets. This can be a great way to meet new people and connect with others who share your interests.

3. Volunteer: Volunteering for a cause that aligns with your values can be a great way to meet like-minded individuals. Look for local organizations that focus on environmental or social causes and offer your time and skills to support their mission.

4. Host a minimalist gathering: Consider hosting a minimalist gathering in your home or community space. This could be a potluck, book club, or even a clothing swap. This can be a great way to connect with others, share experiences, and build a sense of community.

Having a supportive community can also help you stay accountable and motivated in your minimalist journey. You can share your progress, challenges, and successes with others, and learn from their experiences as well. Don't be afraid to reach out and connect with others – you might be surprised by how many people are on a similar path.

Chapter 5: Minimalist Locations
The benefits of minimalist travel

The concept of minimalist travel is about embracing the essence of travel while minimizing the negative impact on both the environment and our own well-being. It is about taking a more mindful and intentional approach to travel, focusing on quality over quantity and experiences over material possessions.

One of the main benefits of minimalist travel is the ability to fully immerse oneself in the local culture and environment. By traveling with a lighter load, you are more agile and flexible, which allows you to explore off the beaten path destinations, interact with locals, and truly appreciate the natural beauty of your surroundings.

Another benefit of minimalist travel is the reduced environmental impact. By packing light and avoiding excessive consumption, you can minimize your carbon footprint and contribute to sustainable tourism practices. This means choosing eco-friendly transportation, accommodations, and activities that align with your values and beliefs.

Minimalist travel can also have a positive impact on our mental and emotional well-being. By eliminating unnecessary stressors, such as overpacking, excessive planning, or unrealistic expectations, we can focus on being present in the moment and enjoying the journey. This allows us to recharge and connect with ourselves, nature, and the world around us.

In addition, minimalist travel can be more affordable, as it encourages us to be more resourceful and creative in our travel planning. By choosing budget-friendly accommodations, local transportation, and street food, we can stretch our travel budget and have more experiences.

Overall, minimalist travel can help us to cultivate a more meaningful and sustainable approach to travel. By prioritizing experiences and connections over material possessions, we can gain a deeper understanding of ourselves and the world around us while minimizing our impact on the planet.

Embracing slow travel and sustainable tourism

Embracing slow travel and sustainable tourism can be a great way to experience the benefits of minimalist travel while also minimizing your impact on the environment and local communities. Slow travel involves taking the time to truly immerse yourself in a destination, rather than rushing from one tourist site to another. This can allow you to gain a deeper understanding and appreciation of the local culture and way of life.

When it comes to sustainable tourism, the goal is to minimize the negative impacts of travel on the environment and local communities while maximizing the positive benefits. This can involve staying in eco-friendly accommodations, supporting local businesses and initiatives, and being mindful of your consumption and waste.

One way to embrace slow travel and sustainable tourism is to choose destinations and activities that align with these values. This might mean staying in a locally-owned guesthouse rather than a big chain hotel, or choosing to explore a natural park on foot or by bike rather than taking a tour bus. It can also mean being mindful of your consumption and waste, such as bringing a refillable water bottle and avoiding single-use plastics.

Another aspect of sustainable tourism is being respectful of local communities and their way of life. This might mean learning some of the local language, being mindful of dress codes and cultural practices, and avoiding activities that exploit animals or people. By making an effort to understand and appreciate the local culture and community, you can create a more meaningful and authentic travel experience while also minimizing your impact on the environment and local people.

Overall, embracing slow travel and sustainable tourism can be a rewarding way to experience the benefits of minimalist travel while also supporting local communities and protecting the environment for future generations to enjoy.

Packing light and reducing waste while traveling

Packing light and reducing waste while traveling are two key principles of minimalist travel. By packing light, you can move through your journey with greater ease and reduce the environmental impact of your travel. Here are some tips to help you pack light and reduce waste while traveling:

1. Plan ahead: Start by making a packing list and prioritizing the essentials. Consider the climate and the activities you have planned for your trip. This will help you avoid overpacking and ensure that you have everything you need.

2. Choose versatile clothing: Select clothing items that can be mixed and matched to create different outfits. Choose fabrics that are lightweight and quick-drying, making it easier to wash and dry your clothes while traveling.

3. Use a carry-on bag: Opt for a carry-on bag instead of a large suitcase. This will limit the amount of space you have to pack and ensure that you can move through airports and train stations more easily.

4. Pack reusable items: Bring reusable items such as a water bottle, travel utensils, and a cloth shopping bag. This will reduce your dependence on disposable items while traveling.

5. Minimize toiletries: Pack only the essentials when it comes to toiletries. Bring travel-sized containers and refill them as needed along the way. Consider using solid toiletries such as shampoo bars and soap bars to avoid liquid restrictions on flights.

6. Leave room for souvenirs: If you plan to bring home souvenirs, leave some extra space in your bag for them. Alternatively, consider shipping them home to avoid excess baggage fees.

Reducing waste while traveling is also important. Here are some tips to help you minimize your environmental impact while on the road:

1. Bring a reusable water bottle: Use a reusable water bottle instead of buying bottled water. This will reduce the amount of plastic waste you generate.

2. Avoid single-use plastics: Avoid single-use plastics such as straws, plastic bags, and plastic cutlery. Bring your own reusable alternatives instead.

3. Use public transportation: Choose public transportation over renting a car or taking taxis. This will reduce your carbon footprint and help support local communities.

4. Eat local and plant-based: Opt for local and plant-based food options. This will reduce the environmental impact of your meals and support the local economy.

5. Stay at eco-friendly accommodations: Look for eco-friendly accommodations such as hotels with green certifications or locally-owned guesthouses. These accommodations are often more sustainable and environmentally friendly.

By embracing the principles of minimalist travel, you can reduce your environmental impact while enjoying a more fulfilling and stress-free travel experience.

Exploring new places with a minimalist mindset

Exploring new places with a minimalist mindset can enhance your travel experience and make it more fulfilling. Minimalist travel is not just about packing light or reducing waste; it is also about exploring new places with a sense of purpose and intentionality. Here are some tips to help you explore new places with a minimalist mindset:

1. Do your research: Before you go, research the place you plan to visit. Find out what makes it unique and what you want to see and experience while you're there. This will help you make the most of your time and avoid tourist traps.

2. Travel light: Packing light is essential for minimalist travel. Bring only what you need and avoid bringing too many things that will weigh you down. This will help you move around more easily and save you time and money on baggage fees.

3. Slow down and savor the moment: Rather than rushing through your itinerary, take the time to savor the moment and enjoy the experience. Instead of trying to see everything, choose a few things that interest you and spend more time there.

4. Immerse yourself in the local culture: Instead of sticking to tourist hotspots, immerse yourself in the local culture. Eat at local restaurants, attend local events, and

interact with the locals. This will help you gain a deeper understanding of the place you're visiting and make meaningful connections.

5. Embrace simplicity: Embrace simplicity while traveling by focusing on the simple pleasures in life. Take a walk in a park, watch the sunset, or enjoy a local specialty. Simple pleasures can often be the most memorable and fulfilling experiences.

6. Be mindful of your impact: Traveling sustainably is an important part of minimalist travel. Be mindful of your impact on the environment and the local community. Reduce waste by bringing a reusable water bottle and shopping bag, support local businesses, and respect the local culture and traditions.

In conclusion, exploring new places with a minimalist mindset can enhance your travel experience and make it more meaningful. By traveling with intentionality, you can gain a deeper understanding of the place you're visiting and make meaningful connections with the locals. So, pack light, slow down, and embrace simplicity to make the most of your travel experience.

Chapter 6: Minimalist Mindset
Cultivating mindfulness and gratitude in a minimalist lifestyle

Living a minimalist lifestyle can have a significant impact on our overall mindset and well-being. Cultivating mindfulness and gratitude can enhance the minimalist experience by helping us appreciate what we have and find joy in simplicity. Here are some ways to cultivate mindfulness and gratitude in a minimalist lifestyle:

1. Practice gratitude daily: Take a few moments each day to reflect on the things you are grateful for in your life. This can be as simple as expressing gratitude for having a roof over your head, food to eat, or a supportive friend.

2. Embrace simplicity: Simplifying your life can help reduce stress and create space for mindfulness. This can be achieved by decluttering your home, reducing your commitments, and focusing on what truly matters to you.

3. Be present: Mindfulness involves being fully present in the moment and paying attention to your thoughts, feelings, and surroundings without judgment. This can be practiced through meditation, deep breathing exercises, or simply taking a few moments each day to be still and observe your surroundings.

4. Slow down: Our fast-paced society can often lead us to rush through our days without taking the time to appreciate the world around us. Take a break from technology and distractions, and slow down to enjoy the simple pleasures in life.

5. Focus on experiences over possessions: Instead of accumulating more things, focus on creating experiences and memories with loved ones. This can involve traveling to new places, trying new hobbies, or simply spending quality time with family and friends.

6. Let go of perfectionism: Perfectionism can be a major barrier to mindfulness and gratitude. Accepting imperfection and embracing the present moment can help you find more joy and fulfillment in your life.

By embracing a minimalist mindset and practicing mindfulness and gratitude, you can experience greater peace and contentment in your life. Start small by focusing on one or two of these practices, and gradually incorporate them into your daily routine. Over time, you may find that you are able to let go of stress and worry, and find more joy in the simple moments of life.

Embracing simplicity as a form of self-care

Living a minimalist lifestyle is more than just decluttering your physical possessions; it is also about simplifying your life in all aspects, including your mental and emotional well-being. Embracing simplicity can be a form of self-care, and it can have a positive impact on your overall health and happiness.

When you have fewer possessions, you have fewer things to worry about and maintain. This can lead to less stress and more time for self-care activities, such as exercise, meditation, or spending time with loved ones. Additionally, a minimalist mindset can help you prioritize your time and energy on things that truly matter to you, allowing you to focus on your personal growth and well-being.

Simplifying your life also means being intentional with the things you do and the decisions you make. This can lead to a sense of clarity and purpose, which can be empowering and fulfilling. By prioritizing what truly matters to you, you can make more mindful choices and create a life that aligns with your values and goals.

Practicing gratitude is also an important part of a minimalist mindset. Instead of constantly striving for more, take time to appreciate the things you have and the people in your life. By focusing on what you already have, you can find contentment and happiness in the present moment.

Moreover, embracing simplicity as a form of self-care can also lead to financial benefits. By buying and owning less, you can save money and use it to invest in experiences or things that truly matter to you, such as traveling or hobbies. This can also help you avoid the stress and burden of debt, which can have a negative impact on your mental and emotional well-being.

In conclusion, simplifying your life and embracing a minimalist mindset can be a powerful form of self-care. By prioritizing what truly matters to you, practicing gratitude, and being intentional with your time and energy, you can create a life that is fulfilling, peaceful, and aligned with your values and goals.

Overcoming consumerism and the pressure to acquire more

Overcoming consumerism and the pressure to acquire more is an essential aspect of embracing a minimalist lifestyle. Consumerism is a societal norm that encourages people to buy more and more, often leading to unnecessary and excessive consumption. As a result, many people accumulate a vast amount of possessions that do not necessarily bring them happiness or fulfilment.

One of the first steps towards overcoming consumerism is to recognize the negative impact it can have on our lives. The constant pressure to acquire more can create stress, anxiety, and financial difficulties. It can also contribute to environmental problems such as resource depletion and waste generation. By acknowledging the downsides of consumerism, we can start to break free from its grip and begin to appreciate the value of simplicity.

Another helpful approach is to adopt a mindful and intentional mindset towards consumption. This means becoming more aware of what we really need and focusing on the quality rather than quantity of our possessions. By doing so, we can avoid buying things that we do not truly need and start to invest in items that will bring us long-term value and satisfaction.

Decluttering is another essential step in overcoming consumerism. It involves simplifying our possessions and letting go of those that no longer serve a purpose in our lives. Decluttering not only frees up physical space but also mental and emotional space, allowing us to focus on the things that truly matter.

It is also helpful to shift our focus from material possessions to experiences and relationships. Instead of accumulating more things, we can invest in experiences that enrich our lives and create lasting memories. For instance, instead of buying more clothes, we can spend money on travel, cultural events, or activities with loved ones.

Another way to overcome consumerism is to seek out alternatives to traditional consumerist activities. For example, instead of going on a shopping spree, we can spend time outdoors, volunteer in our community, or take up a new hobby. These activities can provide a sense of fulfilment and satisfaction without the need to acquire more material possessions.

In conclusion, overcoming consumerism is an essential step in embracing a minimalist lifestyle. By becoming aware of the negative impact of excessive consumption, adopting a mindful and intentional mindset, decluttering, focusing on experiences and relationships, and seeking out alternatives, we can break free from the pressure to acquire more and live a more fulfilling and sustainable life.

Living with intention and purpose

Living with intention and purpose is a fundamental aspect of the minimalist mindset. It means being mindful of your choices and actions, and aligning them with your values and goals. By doing so, you can create a life that is fulfilling and meaningful, rather than one that is defined by external pressures and expectations.

To live with intention and purpose, it is important to start by identifying your values and what matters most to you. This could involve reflecting on your past experiences, your relationships, your passions, and your goals. Once you have a clear sense of your values, you can start to make choices that align with them.

One way to live with intention and purpose is to set goals that are meaningful to you. These could be short-term or long-term goals, and they could be related to any area of your life, such as your career, your relationships, your health, or your personal growth. By setting goals that align with your values, you can create a sense of purpose and direction in your life.

Another way to live with intention and purpose is to practice mindfulness in your daily life. Mindfulness involves being fully present and aware of your thoughts, feelings, and sensations in the present moment. It can help you to stay grounded and centered, and to make choices that are in line with your values and goals.

Living with intention and purpose also means being intentional about how you spend your time and energy. It means focusing on the things that matter most to you, and letting go of things that are not essential or that drain your energy. This could involve simplifying your schedule, reducing your commitments, and saying no to things that are not in line with your values or goals.

In a minimalist lifestyle, living with intention and purpose can also mean being intentional about the things you own and the things you let into your life. It means being mindful of the impact that your possessions and consumption have on the environment and on others. By being intentional about what you own and what you consume, you can reduce your environmental footprint and live a more sustainable life.

Living with intention and purpose is not always easy, and it requires ongoing reflection and self-awareness. But by doing so, you can create a life that is aligned with your values and that brings you joy and fulfillment.

Chapter 7: Minimalist Parenting
Raising children with a minimalist mindset

Raising children can be a challenging task, and doing so with a minimalist mindset may seem even more daunting. However, adopting a minimalist approach to parenting can have numerous benefits, both for parents and children.

One of the first steps towards minimalist parenting is to evaluate what is truly important. This means taking a closer look at the values and priorities that guide your family's life. Minimalist parenting involves making intentional choices and being mindful of the items and activities you bring into your home and your children's lives. This can mean choosing quality over quantity and focusing on experiences over material possessions.

Creating a minimalist home environment can be a powerful way to foster creativity, imagination, and self-sufficiency in children. Children who grow up in a cluttered or chaotic environment can become overwhelmed and distracted, making it difficult for them to focus or engage in imaginative play. On the other hand, a clean, uncluttered space can encourage children to be more independent, responsible, and imaginative.

Minimalist parenting also involves being mindful of the types of toys and activities you introduce into your child's life. Instead of focusing on buying the latest and greatest toys, consider choosing open-ended toys that allow for imaginative play and creativity. Encourage your children to spend time playing outdoors, exploring nature, and engaging in creative activities like drawing, painting, or building.

Another important aspect of minimalist parenting is teaching children the value of experiences over material possessions. Instead of showering children with gifts and toys, focus on creating meaningful experiences that allow your family to spend time together and create lasting memories. This can involve taking family trips, visiting local attractions, or simply spending time playing games or engaging in other activities together.

Minimalist parenting also involves setting boundaries and being mindful of the media and technology that children are exposed to. In today's digital age, it can be easy for children to become overwhelmed or distracted by technology. Setting limits on screen time and being mindful of the types of media that children are exposed to can help foster a healthier relationship with technology and encourage children to engage in other activities that promote creativity, imagination, and self-sufficiency.

In conclusion, adopting a minimalist approach to parenting can have numerous benefits for both parents and children. By focusing on intentional choices, quality over quantity, and experiences over material possessions, parents can create a home environment that encourages creativity, independence, and imagination. Minimalist parenting involves setting boundaries, being mindful of the types of toys and activities introduced into a child's life, and promoting a healthier relationship with technology.

Simplifying family life and reducing stress

In today's fast-paced world, parenting can be stressful and overwhelming. With so many demands on our time and attention, it can be easy to get caught up in the chaos of daily life. However, adopting a minimalist mindset can help parents simplify their family life and reduce stress.

One way to simplify family life is to prioritize and eliminate unnecessary activities and commitments. It's important to recognize that you don't have to do everything and be everywhere. It's okay to say no to certain activities or events if they don't align with your family's values or goals. By reducing the number of commitments, you'll have more time and energy to focus on the things that truly matter.

Another way to simplify family life is to declutter your home. Clutter can be a major source of stress, so by removing excess possessions, you can create a more peaceful and calming environment. It's important to involve your children in this process and teach them the value of minimalism. Encourage them to let go of toys or clothes they no longer use and donate them to those in need.

In addition to decluttering, it's important to establish routines and systems that work for your family. For example, meal planning and prepping can save time and reduce stress during the week. Creating a family schedule or calendar can also help keep everyone organized and on the same page.

Finally, it's important to prioritize quality time together as a family. This can be as simple as a family game night or a walk in the park. By slowing down and enjoying each other's company, you can create meaningful memories and strengthen your family bonds.

In conclusion, simplifying family life and reducing stress is possible through adopting a minimalist mindset. By prioritizing and eliminating unnecessary commitments, decluttering your home, establishing routines and systems, and prioritizing quality time together, parents can create a more peaceful and enjoyable family life.

Minimalist approaches to parenting and child-rearing

Minimalist approaches to parenting and child-rearing involve simplifying family life and focusing on what is truly important for the well-being of both children and parents. By prioritizing the needs of the family and reducing the clutter and chaos of modern family life, minimalist parenting can create a more peaceful and harmonious home environment.

One key aspect of minimalist parenting is reducing the number of toys and material possessions that children have. Research has shown that too many toys can actually be overwhelming for children, leading to a lack of focus and an inability to engage in deep play. By providing children with a smaller number of high-quality toys, parents can encourage deeper play experiences and help their children develop their creativity and imagination.

Minimalist parenting also involves reducing the amount of scheduled activities and screen time in a child's life. Many modern children are overscheduled with after-school activities and extracurriculars, leaving little time for free play and unstructured time with family and friends. By simplifying their schedules and encouraging unstructured play time, parents can help their children develop important social and emotional skills, such as problem-solving, creativity, and self-regulation.

Another aspect of minimalist parenting is promoting sustainable and eco-friendly practices in the home. By teaching children the importance of reducing waste and conserving resources, parents can help them develop a sense of responsibility and environmental stewardship. This can include practices such as composting, recycling, and reducing plastic consumption.

In addition to simplifying the physical environment and schedule of family life, minimalist parenting also involves cultivating a mindful and intentional approach to parenting. This can involve practices such as setting clear boundaries and expectations, practicing active listening and empathy, and modeling healthy behaviors and attitudes for children to emulate.

Overall, minimalist parenting is about creating a more intentional and mindful approach to family life, focusing on what is truly important and necessary for the well-being of both children and parents. By prioritizing quality time together, reducing material possessions and clutter, and promoting sustainable practices, parents can create a more peaceful and fulfilling family life for everyone involved.

Creating a minimalist home environment for kids

Creating a minimalist home environment for kids can help simplify family life and reduce stress. It's important to remember that children don't need a lot of stuff to be happy and healthy. In fact, an excess of toys and clutter can actually be overwhelming and distracting for young minds. Here are some tips for creating a minimalist home environment for kids:

1. Declutter regularly: Go through your child's toys and clothes regularly and donate or sell anything that they've outgrown or no longer use. This will help keep your home clutter-free and make it easier for your child to find and enjoy the things they truly love.

2. Choose quality over quantity: Instead of buying lots of cheap toys and clothes, invest in high-quality items that will last longer and be more meaningful to your child. For example, one or two well-made wooden toys will likely be more appreciated and played with than a dozen plastic toys that will break easily.

3. Create designated play spaces: Instead of letting toys take over your entire home, create designated play spaces in one or two rooms. This will help contain the clutter and make it easier for your child to focus on playing and learning.

4. Use open storage solutions: Consider using open storage solutions, like baskets or shelves, to store toys and books. This makes it easier for your child to see and access their belongings and encourages them to take ownership of their space.

5. Involve your child in the process: As your child gets older, involve them in the process of decluttering and organizing their belongings. This will help teach them important life skills and encourage them to value experiences over possessions.

Overall, creating a minimalist home environment for kids can help simplify family life and promote a more intentional and mindful approach to parenting. By focusing on quality over quantity and involving your child in the process, you can create a home environment that supports their growth and development while reducing stress and overwhelm for everyone.

Chapter 8: Minimalism and Global Impact
The impact of minimalism on a global scale

Minimalism is not just a lifestyle choice for individuals, but it also has the potential to make a positive impact on the world. In recent years, the concept of minimalism has gained popularity, and more people are becoming aware of the impact of their consumption habits on the environment. In this section, we will explore the ways in which minimalism can contribute to a better world.

Firstly, minimalism encourages people to consume less and reduce waste. When we live with fewer possessions, we are less likely to purchase items that we do not need, leading to a reduction in waste. The idea of using what we have and making do with less has a significant impact on the environment, as it reduces the demand for resources and limits the amount of waste that goes to landfills.

Secondly, minimalism promotes sustainable living. Living a minimalist lifestyle means being intentional with our choices, including the items we buy, the food we eat, and the energy we use. Sustainable living involves making choices that reduce our carbon footprint and minimize harm to the environment. For instance, choosing to walk or bike instead of driving, using reusable containers instead of disposable ones, and consuming locally sourced food are all ways to live sustainably.

Thirdly, minimalism encourages people to donate and share their possessions. Instead of throwing away items we no longer need or want, we can give them away to others who could benefit from them. This can be done through donating to charitable organizations or giving away items to friends or family members. By doing so, we not only reduce waste, but we also help others in need, promoting a sense of community and generosity.

Lastly, minimalism encourages people to be mindful of the impact of their choices on the environment. By being aware of our consumption habits, we can make choices that reduce harm to the environment. This includes choosing products made from sustainable materials, supporting companies that prioritize sustainability, and reducing our energy usage.

In conclusion, minimalism can have a significant impact on the environment, as it encourages people to consume less, live sustainably, donate and share their possessions, and be mindful of their impact on the environment. By adopting a minimalist lifestyle, individuals can contribute to a better world and make a positive impact on the global community.

The benefits of minimalism for the environment globally

Minimalism is not just about reducing clutter and simplifying our lives; it also has a significant impact on the environment. The principles of minimalism, such as reducing waste and consumption, are increasingly relevant in the face of global environmental challenges such as climate change and resource depletion. In this section, we will explore the benefits of minimalism for the environment and how practicing minimalism can make a positive impact globally.

1. Reducing Waste

Minimalism encourages us to buy and consume less, which directly translates to reducing the amount of waste we produce. By opting for reusable items such as water bottles, grocery bags, and cloth napkins, we can reduce the amount of waste we generate. We can also recycle and repurpose items to minimize waste. By reducing waste, we can contribute to reducing landfill pollution and greenhouse gas emissions.

2. Conserving Resources

Minimalism also promotes the conservation of resources such as energy, water, and raw materials. By using energy-efficient appliances and light bulbs, turning off lights when not in use, and reducing water usage, we can conserve natural resources and reduce our environmental impact. Choosing products made from sustainable materials and supporting companies that prioritize environmental sustainability can also contribute to the conservation of resources.

3. Mitigating Climate Change

The principles of minimalism align with the goals of mitigating climate change. By reducing consumption and waste, we can reduce the demand for the production of goods, which can lead to a reduction in greenhouse gas emissions. Additionally, by choosing to walk, bike, or use public transportation instead of driving a car, we can reduce carbon emissions and our carbon footprint. This can contribute to the global effort to limit the rise in global temperatures and mitigate the impacts of climate change.

4. Promoting Sustainability

Minimalism promotes sustainability by encouraging us to live within our means and prioritize our needs over our wants. By doing so, we can reduce the strain on the planet's resources and promote sustainable living. We can also support companies and products that prioritize sustainability and responsible environmental practices. By making small changes in our daily lives, we can contribute to promoting sustainability globally.

5. Inspiring Others

Practicing minimalism can also inspire others to make positive changes in their lives and contribute to the global effort to reduce environmental impact. By leading by example and sharing our experiences and tips for living a minimalist lifestyle, we can inspire others to adopt a more sustainable and mindful way of living. By doing so, we can create a ripple effect that can contribute to a global movement toward sustainability and environmental consciousness.

In conclusion, practicing minimalism has numerous benefits for the environment on a global scale. By reducing waste and consumption, conserving resources, mitigating climate change, promoting sustainability, and inspiring others, we can contribute to a more sustainable and mindful way of living. By making small changes in our daily lives, we can make a positive impact on the environment and create a more sustainable future for ourselves and generations to come.

The impact of consumerism on developing countries

Consumerism is a lifestyle that revolves around the acquisition and consumption of material goods and services. While it has been embraced by many as a means of achieving happiness and fulfillment, it has also had a profound impact on the environment and on developing countries around the world.

The rise of consumerism has led to the depletion of natural resources and the generation of a massive amount of waste. This has had a negative impact on the environment, including pollution, deforestation, and climate change. In addition, the production of goods and services required to satisfy consumer demand often involves the exploitation of labor and resources in developing countries, leading to social and economic inequality.

Developing countries are often the source of raw materials used in the production of consumer goods. The extraction of these resources can have a devastating impact on the environment and on the communities that depend on them for their livelihoods. In many cases, the profits from these resources do not benefit the local population, but instead are siphoned off by corrupt officials or foreign investors.

The production of consumer goods also often involves the exploitation of labor in developing countries. Workers are often paid low wages, work in dangerous conditions, and have limited or no access to basic rights and protections. This has led to the creation of sweatshops and other forms of exploitative labor practices, which perpetuate poverty and inequality.

The impact of consumerism on developing countries is not just limited to the production of goods. It also affects the way in which these countries are viewed by the rest of the world. Many developed countries view developing countries as sources of cheap labor and raw materials, rather than as partners in sustainable development. This mindset perpetuates a cycle of exploitation and inequality, making it difficult for developing countries to break free from the cycle of poverty and environmental degradation.

Minimalism offers a different approach. By prioritizing the essentials and avoiding unnecessary consumption, we can reduce our impact on the environment and help to break the cycle of exploitation and inequality. This means reducing waste, using resources responsibly, and supporting sustainable practices. It also means being mindful of the impact of our choices on the world around us, and taking action to reduce our contribution to the problem.

By embracing minimalism, we can also shift our mindset away from the constant pursuit of material possessions and towards a focus on what really matters – our relationships, our experiences, and our contributions to the world. This can help to break the cycle of consumerism and encourage a more sustainable and equitable way of life for all.

The intersection of minimalism and social justice globally

The minimalist lifestyle is often associated with personal benefits such as reduced stress, improved well-being, and increased financial security. However, minimalist principles can also intersect with broader social justice issues on a global scale.

One of the key areas where minimalism intersects with social justice is through ethical consumption. In a global economy where production is often outsourced to developing countries with lower labor standards and environmental regulations, our consumption patterns can have far-reaching consequences. By practicing minimalism, we can reduce our overall consumption, become more mindful of our purchasing choices, and prioritize ethical and sustainable options.

Another way in which minimalism can intersect with social justice is through addressing income inequality. Minimalism often emphasizes the idea of living with less, but this can also mean reducing the gap between those who have excess and those who are struggling to make ends meet. By reducing our own consumption and redirecting resources towards supporting social causes, we can contribute to a more equitable distribution of resources on a global scale.

Minimalism can also intersect with environmental justice, particularly when it comes to issues such as climate change and pollution. The overconsumption of resources and reliance on fossil fuels in developed countries has contributed significantly to global climate change, while the impacts of these changes are often felt most acutely in developing countries with limited resources and infrastructure to cope with the effects.

By embracing a minimalist lifestyle, we can reduce our overall environmental impact, contribute to the reduction of carbon emissions, and support sustainable practices. This can be achieved through actions such as reducing our use of single-use plastics, choosing public transportation over driving, and supporting environmentally-friendly products and practices.

Minimalism can also intersect with social justice issues through the promotion of community and collaboration. In a world where individualism and consumerism are often prioritized, minimalism emphasizes the importance of relationships and connection. By focusing on building community and supporting local initiatives, we can contribute to the creation of more resilient and sustainable societies.

Overall, the practice of minimalism has the potential to intersect with a wide range of social justice issues on a global scale. By reducing our consumption, redirecting resources towards ethical and sustainable options, and promoting community and collaboration, we can contribute to a more just and equitable world.

Conclusion

The benefits of minimalism for individuals and the environment

As we come to the end of this book, it's important to reflect on the many benefits that adopting a minimalist lifestyle can bring. Not only can it lead to a more fulfilling and intentional way of living, but it can also have a positive impact on the environment and society as a whole.

One of the most obvious benefits of minimalism is the reduction in physical clutter and possessions. By simplifying our lives and focusing on what truly matters, we can reduce stress and anxiety, and create a more peaceful and calming home environment. This can also lead to better mental health and well-being, as we become more mindful of our choices and how they impact our lives.

Minimalism can also have a positive impact on the environment. By reducing our consumption and waste, we can help to conserve resources and reduce the carbon footprint of our daily lives. This can include choosing to buy products with less packaging, using reusable containers and bags, and adopting a more sustainable approach to food and transportation.

Another benefit of minimalism is the opportunity to live a more intentional life. By simplifying our schedules and commitments, we can focus on the things that truly matter to us, whether it be spending time with loved ones, pursuing a hobby or passion, or contributing to our community in a meaningful way. This can lead to a greater sense of purpose and fulfillment, and a more satisfying way of life.

On a broader level, minimalism can also have a positive impact on society as a whole. By reducing our consumption and waste, we can help to address issues such as climate change and environmental degradation, and promote a more sustainable and equitable future. In addition, by focusing on what truly matters in life, we can shift away from a culture of consumerism and materialism, and create a more balanced and fulfilling society.

Of course, adopting a minimalist lifestyle isn't always easy, and it requires a certain degree of commitment and sacrifice. But the benefits that it can bring, both for individuals and for society as a whole, make it a worthwhile pursuit. By taking small steps towards simplifying our lives and reducing our impact on the environment, we can all make a positive difference in the world.

In conclusion, minimalism is much more than just a trend or a fad. It's a powerful mindset and way of life that can lead to greater happiness, purpose, and sustainability. Whether you're just starting out on your minimalist journey or are already well on your way, I hope that this book has provided you with the inspiration and tools to continue living a more intentional and fulfilling life.

The challenges and potential pitfalls of a minimalist lifestyle

As with any significant lifestyle change, adopting a minimalist mindset and embracing minimalism as a way of life comes with its challenges and potential pitfalls. While minimalism can offer numerous benefits, it is essential to consider the difficulties that may arise when implementing this lifestyle.

One of the most significant challenges of minimalism is the temptation to acquire new possessions. Consumerism is deeply ingrained in our culture, and it can be challenging to resist the allure of new and shiny things. Even when we recognize that we don't need something, we may still be drawn to it. It is crucial to cultivate the self-awareness and discipline necessary to resist these urges and remain committed to the minimalist lifestyle.

Another potential pitfall of minimalism is the pressure to declutter and downsize. While decluttering can be freeing and liberating, it can also be overwhelming and stressful. It is essential to approach decluttering with a measured and thoughtful mindset and to recognize that it is a process that takes time. We must also avoid falling into the trap of minimalism as a competition or a race to see who can own the least amount of possessions.

One of the challenges of minimalism is that it can be difficult to balance the desire for simplicity and the need for functionality. Sometimes, minimalist aesthetics can come at the expense of practicality, and it is essential to strike a balance between the two. It is also important to recognize that minimalism may not be the right choice for everyone. We all have different lifestyles, needs, and circumstances, and what works for one person may not work for another.

Another potential challenge of minimalism is the impact it can have on our relationships. Our possessions can hold significant emotional value, and letting go of them can be difficult. We may also face criticism and pushback from friends and family who don't understand or share our values. It is essential to communicate our intentions and motivations clearly and respectfully, to listen to the perspectives of others, and to be open to compromise and flexibility.

In conclusion, while minimalism can offer numerous benefits, it is essential to approach this lifestyle with a measured and thoughtful mindset. We must recognize the challenges and potential pitfalls and work to cultivate the self-awareness, discipline, and balance necessary to navigate them successfully. Ultimately, the decision to embrace minimalism is a deeply personal one, and it is up to each of us to determine what works best for our individual circumstances and needs.

Final thoughts on embracing minimalism for a happier, more sustainable life

As we come to the end of this book on minimalism, it's important to reflect on the key takeaways and final thoughts about how embracing minimalism can lead to a happier, more sustainable life.

Minimalism is not just about decluttering or getting rid of possessions. It's about intentionally choosing to live with less in order to focus on what truly matters in life. By minimizing our possessions, we can minimize our stress and increase our overall sense of wellbeing.

One of the main benefits of minimalism is that it allows us to be more mindful and intentional in our choices. We become more aware of our consumption habits, which helps us reduce our impact on the environment. By consuming less, we can also save money and live a more sustainable lifestyle.

However, embracing minimalism is not always easy. It requires us to break away from societal expectations and reevaluate our values and priorities. It can be challenging to let go of possessions that we may have sentimental attachments to or that we have been conditioned to believe we need.

Another potential pitfall of minimalism is that it can become an obsession, leading to perfectionism and an unhealthy attachment to the idea of minimalism itself. It's important to remember that minimalism is a tool, not a goal. We should strive to live intentionally and thoughtfully, but not become so focused on minimalism that it becomes an end in itself.

In conclusion, embracing minimalism can lead to a happier, more sustainable life. By focusing on what truly matters and intentionally choosing to live with less, we can reduce our stress, increase our mindfulness, and have a positive impact on the environment. However, it's important to be aware of the potential challenges and pitfalls of minimalism, and to approach it with a balanced and thoughtful mindset. By doing so, we can create a life that is truly fulfilling and meaningful.

THE END

Key Terms and Definitions

To help you better understand the language and concepts related to aging and older adults, below you will find a list of key terms and their definitions.

1. Minimalism: A lifestyle characterized by living with fewer possessions and a focus on simplicity and mindfulness.

2. Decluttering: The process of removing unnecessary or unused items from one's home or life.

3. Simplicity: The state or quality of being simple, characterized by a lack of complexity, ornamentation, or excess.

4. Mindfulness: The practice of being present and fully engaged in the current moment, without distraction or judgment.

5. Consumerism: The belief that the acquisition of goods and services is a desirable and necessary component of a successful and fulfilling life.

6. Sustainability: The ability to maintain a certain level of ecological, economic, and social balance over time, without depleting natural resources or causing harm to the environment.

7. Intentionality: The act of making deliberate and purposeful choices, rather than acting on impulse or without forethought.

8. Gratitude: The quality of being thankful or appreciative, often expressed towards others or for one's own life circumstances.

9. Mindset: A person's attitudes, beliefs, and values that shape their perception of the world and their behavior within it.

10. Parenting: The act of raising and caring for children, including providing guidance, support, and nurturing.

11. Environment: The natural world and the systems and conditions that exist within it.

12. Global Impact: The influence or effect of an action or behavior on a global scale, often related to environmental or social issues.

Supporting Materials

Introduction:

Becker, J. (2010). Simplicity: Essays. Createspace Independent Publishing.

Sasaki, F. (2015). Goodbye, Things: The New Japanese Minimalism. W.W. Norton & Company.

Chapter 1: Minimalist Living

Millburn, J. F., & Nicodemus, R. (2011). Minimalism: Live a Meaningful Life. Asymmetrical Press.

Jay, M. (2016). The Joy of Less: A Minimalist Guide to Declutter, Organize, and Simplify. Chronicle Books.

Chapter 2: Minimalist Eating

Sasaki, F. (2017). The Minimalist Baker's Everyday Cooking: 101 Entirely Plant-based, Mostly Gluten-Free, Easy and Delicious Recipes. Penguin Random House.

Flanders, J. (2016). The Zero Waste Cookbook: 100 Recipes for Cooking Without Waste. Ten Speed Press.

Chapter 3: Minimalist Materials

Becker, J. (2010). Simplicity: Essays. Createspace Independent Publishing.

Johnson, B. (2016). The Zero Waste Home: 101 Ways to Reduce Waste and Save Money in Your Home. Simon & Schuster.

Chapter 4: Minimalist People

Sasaki, F. (2015). Goodbye, Things: The New Japanese Minimalism. W.W. Norton & Company.

Becker, J. (2010). Simplicity: Essays. Createspace Independent Publishing.

Chapter 5: Minimalist Locations

Foster, J. B., & McChesney, R. W. (2014). The Endless Crisis: How Monopoly-Finance Capital Produces Stagnation and Upheaval from the USA to China. Monthly Review Press.

Sasaki, F. (2015). Goodbye, Things: The New Japanese Minimalism. W.W. Norton & Company.

Chapter 6: Minimalist Mindset

Millburn, J. F., & Nicodemus, R. (2011). Minimalism: Live a Meaningful Life. Asymmetrical Press.

Sasaki, F. (2015). Goodbye, Things: The New Japanese Minimalism. W.W. Norton & Company.

Chapter 7: Minimalist Parenting

Sadowsky, J. (2013). Minimalist Parenting: Enjoy Modern Family Life More by Doing Less. Bibliomotion, Inc.

Kuo, Y. (2018). The More of Less: Finding the Life You Want Under Everything You Own. B&H Publishing Group.

Chapter 8: Minimalism and Global Impact

Kuo, Y. (2018). The More of Less: Finding the Life You Want Under Everything You Own. B&H Publishing Group.

Sadowsky, J. (2013). Minimalist Parenting: Enjoy Modern Family Life More by Doing Less. Bibliomotion, Inc.
Conclusion
Millburn, J. F., & Nicodemus, R. (2011). Minimalism: Live a Meaningful Life. Asymmetrical Press.
Sasaki, F. (2015). Goodbye, Things: The New Japanese Minimalism. W.W. Norton & Company.

www.ingramcontent.com/pod-product-compliance
Lightning Source LLC
Chambersburg PA
CBHW070644030426
42337CB00020B/4155